LOVE...*an experience of*

love

Peter

By the same author

COME LOVE WITH ME AND BE MY LIFE

I HAVE LOVED

FOR LOVERS AND NO OTHERS

I LOVE THEREFORE I AM

THE HARD STUFF: LOVE

EVOLVING AT THE SPEED OF LOVE

SURVIVING THE LOSS OF A LOVE

the above books published by
Versemonger Press
5806 Elizabeth Court
Allen Park, Michigan
48101

Love

...an experience of

Peter McWilliams

DOUBLEDAY & COMPANY, INC., GARDEN CITY, NEW YORK, 1972

Library of Congress Catalog Card Number 75–184919
Copyright © 1972 by Peter McWilliams
Printed in the United States of America
First Edition

LOVE
. . . AN EXPERIENCE OF

LOVE...*an experience of*

I
*Come. Become a linguist
with me.*

what I feel
cannot be termed
loneliness or pain
or depression. . . .

it's more an
overall lack
of intensity
in all
emotions,
functions,
relationships.

I guess I have
"the blahs."

maybe I should
take an
alka seltzer.

How will it happen?
How will it happen
when I find some
someone to spend
a goodly portion
of my life with?

It must happen. . . .
I mean, I've been
pre-pairing
so long. . . .

It will happen.
yes.

I will not dwell on
if,
only
how, when, where, whom.

running from people
who want me who I want
nothing to do with

while

running after people
who I want who want
nothing to do with me,

I have lost all the
perspective
I never had.

I reach out to people
and I Touch them
and they respond.

they respond.
they just respond.

Oh god,
how I need someone
to reach out to me.

this is a
simple
statement
of
loneliness.

a simpler
statement
would be a
scream.

I tried that,
but found it
lacking in
literary
merit.

I summoned up
the devil within
me and I
said:

"I will sell
you my soul.
what will you
give me for
It?"

my devil smiled
(I didn't
deserve a laugh)
and replied:

"Why should I
make an offer
for something
I already own?"

Oh Lady,
with your
oils and
edible wildflower roots
and salves and
1967 San Franciscan
miss conception
of what
     human
     beauty
is all about,

I could never love you.

waiting for a
love partner
is difficult
because there
is no one to
wait with.

my phone book
is an
encyclopedia
of people who
don't want to
talk to me or
who I don't want
to talk to or
both.

and I don't think
my name is in
anybody's phone book
. . . except the telephone company's.

Everybody else has one
Why can't I?

"too old"
"too young"
"too busy"
"too lazy"
"too happy"
"too sad"
"too good"
"too bad"

why can't I be
too something to
help me ignore my
need to love?

it's hard to love when
those that preach can't practice
and those that practice don't teach.

if the bible
is anything to
go by, God is
not a romantic.

He punished
Adam for doing
Eve's bidding.

I would have
rewarded him.

keep the
"found"
in
profound.

keep the
"fun"
in
profundity.

sex is a tool of
communication,

just as a

saw is a tool of
carpentry.

if you pound
nails with a
saw you won't
be able to
cut down many
trees.

Vicarious
living is
dead.

a lost last love
who last year I almost
killed myself over called
and wanted to talk to me
but I was so anxious to see
you
I said I didn't have time and
hung up.

One year later.
I didn't have time.

One week later.
You don't have time.

Your metabolism is
much faster than mine.

the right
"combination of ingredients"
as they say on the Bufferin commercial.

wit
beauty
intelligence

and strangely enough this
neat combination
cares for
me
(!)

but this
neat combination
also cares
for another
neat combination
with whom the
neat combination
lives.

not so neat.

I think I'll take
a Bufferin.

all night long.

laughing.
playing with words
pillows blankets time
eachother.

falling in love.
falling asleep.

not making love
until the next
morning and the
birds were singing

you smile.
I forget where I am.
and it takes me longer
each time to remember again.

I don't think
I'll call you
tonight.

I'll take on
another activity
and loose myself
in busy-ness.

you're begining to mean
too much
to me

and I still don't
know how to
handle that

I know
I love you.

I do not know
which one of us
those words scare
most.

I want to
delve the depths
of
one to one
human emotion
with you.

I want to say
whatever words
need be said
to get words
out of the way.

I am impatient.
I am frightened.
I am anticipatory.
I am in love with you.

your
imperfections
only draw me
closer to you.

They remind me
that you're
human.

that with humans
I have a chance.

I would like to
know you.
Know you well.

your concepts . . .
where they came from.
where they are taking you.

what it is
that makes
you . . . you.

I already like you.
I'd like to know why.

An intellectual puzzle.
no, not really: a journey.

and since I already
know what lies at
the farthest reach
of your mind,
I will enjoy
the traveling
all the more.

my first impressions
aren't very
impressive
of late.

But I am not concerned.

those who
know know
it's love.

those who
don't, I
don't care
to know.

talk
is the language of
friends.

touch
is the language of
loves.

come.
become a
linguist
with me.

II

A Few Facts of Life:

Earthquakes level large cities

Birds lay eggs

Ice is cold

An orange is orange

Dogs bark

Fire is hot

Bees fly

I love you

Sea water contains salt

Crocodiles have sharp teeth

Flowers grow

Books are made of paper.

III

I had all but forgotten this feeling

I had all but
forgotten
this feeling.
a
survival mechanism
at work, no doubt.

somehow the months
have constructed a
mental image of
painless love.

Ha!

I write this poem
to remind me of
these hours, and
all those that
have preceded
them.

the months will
not play such a
cruel trick on
me again . . .

although the
years might.

Those who Know
have known no.

an oyster's
tears turn
to pearls.

a poet's
tears turn
to poems.

there
is no
logic
to my
needs
my
love. . . .

well, not
any that
you
would understand.

saying
good night
you
leave,
sentencing
me to a
bad
one.

grief,
be brief.

pain,
refrain.

alone,
go home.

fear,
disappear.

rhymes,
another time.

this sickness
I call love.

I have it for you.

I can't blame you
for not wanting it,

I don't want it
myself.

That's why I
give it so freely
to people who don't
have any of their own.

searching for gold
I tunneled into you.

there was a cave-in.

I am crushed.

Hermann Hesse, from *Steppenwolf:*

"The man of power is ruined
by power, the man of money
by money, the submissive man
by subservience, the pleasure
seeker by pleasure . . ."

and me,
by love.

pain
    is not so heavy
    a burden in the
    summer.

walks
    through
    travelogue scenes
    prevent a good
    deal of destruction.

and
    even though no one
    is there to warm me,
    the sun will.

but
    Fall just fell,
    leaving Winter,
    and me
    with no warmth
    within to face
    the cold without.

I might just stick
to the sidewalk
and freeze.

excuse me

I am currently afflicted with the world's
number one cripplier

INFATUATION FIXATION PARALYSIS

commonly refered to in non-medical circles as

LOVE

any spare COMFORT you have to give would be
most appreciated, although my ability to re-
cieve may be temporally impaired.

thank you

IIII

*Pain is loving
an objecting object*

pain
is
the
presence
of
your
absence

pain
is
what
I'm
in
when
you're
out

pain
is
eating
the
food
alone
we
grew
together

pain
is
my
love
doing
something
I
like
without
me

pain
is
you
and
me
not
making
we

pain
is
the
call
that
never
came

pain
is
no
when
I
need
yes

pain
is
yes
when
I
need
no

pain
is
love
felt
but
not
shared

pain
is
what
I
share
with
myself
when
we
aren't
sharing
each
other

pain
is
what
burns
when
there's
no
love
to
warm

pain
is
loving
an
objecting
object

pain
is
when
time
out-
numbers
rhymes

pain
is
discovering
there
is
nothing
left
to
discover

pain
is
better
than
no
feeling
at
all

pain
is
the
sane's
taste
of
insanity

pain
is
joy's
vacation

and
my
vocation

pain
is
terminal
loneliness

pain
is

and
I
often
wish
it
wasn't

pain
is
care
when
there's
no
one
there

pain
is
the
rigor
mortis
of
a
dead
love

pain
is
a
beautiful
day
and
no
one
to
share
it
with

pain
is
any
thought
of
our
joy
together
now
that
we're
apart

pain
is
a
mind
that
is
not
only
closed
but
locked

pain
is
where
I
am
until
I
love
again

Pain
is
not
being
able
to
love
even
god.

V
I find I lost

at first my love for you seemed the
most important force in the universe.

for a while
I loved you well
& it made me well.
("energy flowing through a
    system acts to organize
    that system.")

the giving of love was so
joyous
I wanted you too to experience
this joy.

So I asked you
to love me

an impossibility . . .
that turned into a goal
that turned into a pain
that drove me insane,
again.

my needs return.
they render me helpless.

and my love for you
seems the most
impotent
force in the universe.

I ask myself
What will I do
if you return.

but that isn't
the question.

The question is
what do I do
now that you're
  gone.

I find
I lost.

warm
human
soft
next to me in the dark
naked
body
together
in a
not necessarily
but
not necessarily not
sexual
situation.

a human want

a want I need

since you
left
me

bleeding.

"needing"
and
"bleeding"
rhyme.

On paper,
and in

reality.

It's
dangerous
to leave a
lonely man
alone.

you don't
know what
lies
he'll tell
about you.

or worse,

what truths.

Keep me alive

too late

I just died.

When I
create
something
it doesn't
hurt
as much.

Maybe
that's why
God
created me.

a new morning
of a
new life
without
you.

so what?

there will be others.
much finer.
much mine-er.

and until then
there is me.

and because I treated
you
well,
I like me better.

also, the sun rises.

I hope I heal soon.

I want to enjoy
autumn.

VI
I will sin again

My sin is loving.
I confess.

My penance is losing.
I accept.

My penance is painful,
but I will sin again.

An Attempt to be Enthusiastic without Being Evangelistic

For years I wandered about life, looking for some stabilizing force, a constant that, once found, would bring peace, security and happiness. I sought my constant in others, in drugs, in Zen, in eating this and none of that, in books, in psychoanalysis and in writing poetry. No luck. Eventually I realized that if it were my constant I would have to look for it within myself. No red-hot, new philosophical thought there, but it was mine. I learned a technique, a process, by which this inner being could be reached, effortlessly and automatically, and since that time the results in my own life space have been amazing.

The technique is called Transcendental Meditation. The term is very misleading. It smacks of mysticism, pretzel positions, ouija boards, mind control, concentration, alien religious traditions, years of exhaustive study and brown rice. Actually it has nothing to do with any of these. Transcendental Meditation (TM) is, simply, an effortless process which allows the mind to come in direct contact with one's own life force, and allows this force to enhance one's living.

Even that sounds mystical. Rather than try to put words around a necessarily wordless experience, let's talk about the mechanics of the technique and its results.

The process is effortless. TM does itself through you. There is no concentration, contemplation, puzzles to solve or songs to sing. The process is automatic. Simply begin the technique and sit quietly. All is done for you, spontaneously. The technique takes fifteen minutes to learn. There are thousands of qualified teachers of TM in the United States alone. The technique cannot be outlined in a book because slight variations are made for each individual. Since all people are not the same, the exact same technique cannot work for all people. Hence, personalized instruction.

There are no Don't's connected with meditation. No "Don't eat meat," no "Don't have sex." No Don't's. There are no complicated Do's, either. No "DO wear this," no "DO love your neighbor," no "DO this exercise." There is but one DO. DO MEDITATE. Twice a day, for about twenty minutes each sitting, Do Meditate. All other times, forget about meditation. Life will grow a quality of its own, on its own. "Don't push the river."

The technique I refer to is called most properly: Transcendental Meditation as taught by Maharishi Mahesh Yogi. As the turn-of-the-century ads proclaimed: "Accept No Substitute!"

As I meditate more, I find life freer, more enjoyable, less stressful. I can love with less fear-pain-desolation than I ever thought possible. The changes within me are subtle yet profound. I feel an all-pervading support for all my actions and thoughts. This TM stuff works.

Maybe love without pain is waiting for me to experience her.

Perhaps Nature saves her greatest gifts until we are fully
grown.

The address of the TM center near you can be obtained by
writing to:
International Meditation Society (IMS)
1015 Gayley Avenue
Los Angeles, California
90024.